© 2021 Robert Chomany Books. All Rights Reserved.

All rights reserved. No part of this publication may be reproduced, distributed, or transmitted in any form or by any means, including photocopying, recording, or other electronic or mechanical methods, without the prior written permission of the publisher, except in the case of brief quotations embodied in critical reviews and certain other noncommercial uses permitted by copyright law.

Developmental Editor: Rachel Small
Copy editing: Author Connections, LLC
Cover image by: Mary Jo Photography

Thank you for your support of the author's rights.

ISBN: 978-1-926518-08-4 (Paperback)
ISBN: 978-1-926518-07-7 (Hardback)
ISBN: 978-1-926518-06-0 (Ebook)

The creative work I do, the writing and the books I put together are dedicated to my mom, because I believe it was her guidance, her love, and her patience that allowed me to find the path I am walking. She showed me how to see with the eyes of my soul and find the beauty that is... life.

Contents

Reflect 1

Look In the Mirror 19

Face the Fear 33

Find Peace 46

Move Forward 61

Communication 82

Sharing 99

Friendship 116

Differences 135

Compassion 151

Inspiration 165

Acknowledgements 184

About the Author 188

Today I say hello to me
hello to my own heart,
hello to the me I love to be
hello to this day's start.
Today I am unique out there
today I am one of a kind
today I am me and proud to be
and today a smile I'll find.

WI:)ND

Reflect

The ability to reflect on things is an acquired strength. To look back on the past without being consumed by it requires an open mind. It is an opportunity to review what we've done, lessons we've learned, and perhaps the reasons why smiles or frowns are attached to particular memories.

The best thing about reflection is that, like a pool of calm water we can peer into, it gives us a chance to see ourselves—who we are and what we've become. Reflection gives us a chance to remember moments and experiences, both difficult and easy times that have helped to shape us, directly and indirectly. To reflect means also to pause, to stop what you're doing and immerse your mind in the energy of people, places, and things—in sights, sounds, and smells that evoke emotional responses: tears, smiles, laughter, or thoughtful peace.

Is there a difference between reflecting and remembering? I think so, because I believe that reflecting on something also means to question it, to recall the motives of a decision or justify a choice. It might involve considering what could have happened if other choices had been made, and appreciating the actual outcomes of events.

Hopefully the memories stirred by reflection are good ones, but the unpleasant ones sometimes lie dormant in our minds (or in our hearts), forgotten if left undisturbed. Reflecting, though, gives us the opportunity to purge, to cleanse our souls and empty the spaces those unpleasant memories fill. We remember why we felt hurt, we thank the universe for lessons learned, and we can then cast the negative feelings to the wind.

Lessons learned through memories can be filed under Do Not Repeat. They won't be there to hamper positive manifestations in the future. Take time to find calm moments when you can ponder the peaceful places in your mind—the spots you travel to when stress causes you to lose balance. Positive contemplation attached to creative imagination is the easiest way to find your focus and serene balance at any moment, day or night.

Walk your path with a casual step
see the footprints you're leaving behind.
When you stop to reflect on how far you've come
there's a smile you will find.

Wherever you are in the world today
whenever your focus is clear
take a moment or two to reflect on life
and the things that you hold dear.
Cherish them for they are real
and they will help you while you're growing,
let these things create the smiles
that you're always happy showing.

Robert Chomany

Maybe it's time you give it some thought
reflect on what's happened of late
like that smile you got or the praise you have sought
or a subtle twisting of fate.
Each moment is new, each challenge too,
at the end there's always a light,
find the tunnel and follow it through,
your effort reflects what's right.

Opportunities for you can be made in your mind,
if you build your own door, then you know what you'll find.

Robert Chomany

Never underestimate the power of positive thought,
it turns things that you want into things that you've got.

Life happens quickly, for some it's too fast,
in fact there are times it's unseen.
Find balance between the things that are coming
and the things that have already been.

Robert Chomany

When a moment comes that finds your heart
let it nestle firmly there,
so later when you need a smile
that moment you can share.

Think about taking a moment or two
to process the day's events,
there doesn't have to be anything wrong
to muse upon smiles you've sent.

The moon is like your quiet soul
it shares its silvery light,
it shines on clouds floating in the sky
and illuminates the night.
Your soul is the essence of who you are
if ever you take time to look,
it always speaks the truth of you
like words that are set in a book.

Robert Chomany

When you amble across the beach of life
see your footprints and reflect,
upon all your thoughts and memories
and the lessons you respect.

Life is a river it flows right on by,
quite often so quietly it mirrors the sky.
The gift of reflection is more powerful it seems,
when we have a rare chance to sit near a stream.
All thoughts and memories become perfectly clear,
when set into motion with water that's near.
Our energy dances amid currents made white,
as the water shares laughter and gives life a new light.

Robert Chomany

Wherever you are, whatever you're doing,
when your day is almost done,
take one more moment just for yourself,
and share a smile with the sun.

Robert Chomany

These minutes that pass all come in groups
of days and months and years,
until you have lived a lifetime filled
with laughter, learning, and tears.
Relive the moments that were filled with joy
and you will smile when you do,
learn from the sadness that some memories bring,
those will build strength in you.

Robert Chomany

Look In the Mirror

What do you see when you look in the mirror? Do you see who you really are? Does the person looking back intimidate you? Are you at ease with the reflection? Have you ever looked in the mirror and felt that the person standing there in front of you was a stranger?

It's common these days to dislike the person you see in the mirror because of pressures created by a demanding society and a biased Internet. Body size and shape are dictated by magazines that have perfected the art of retouching and lying to us, the consumers. They simply mold images of people into their versions of perfection. Preposterous!

Young and old, so many of us avoid truly looking in the mirror—afraid we won't see what we think we're supposed to look like. We often look at ourselves and see only flaws, according to society's perception of how a human being should look.

Enough already. The mirror is your friend. It shows you who you are in your imperfect perfection, presenting an image that no other living thing on the planet could ever accomplish. The mirror is your escape to reality, the place you can go to smile and appreciate those character lines earned from laughter shared while you were experiencing life. The mirror will show the soft curves that time has added to your body because you are happy and healthy. The lines of your silhouette are the lines of a vital human being who is alive and happy to be that way.

Look in the mirror today and see the you that the world sees—the you that shares smiles and strength. Take notice of the energy your soul creates. This is the unique aura that makes you who you are. Recognize and appreciate all you have become, as you look back at you . . . in the mirror.

> The person you see in the mirror today
> is the person you must love to be.
> Your world will be a better place
> when you honor the you that you see.

I like the way you make me feel,
I like the way you look,
I like the way you know me well,
and read me like a book.
The you of course is the one I see
the one in the mirror looking back at me,
the one who means the world to some,
the one of a kind that I have become.

Robert Chomany

If you ever feel the need to change
based on what you've heard,
remember just how important it is
to believe these simple words:
"It's me I see when I look at myself
and I think I am just fine,
I'm proud to be the me I've become,
I like the way I shine."

The stress that you feel just trying to BE
is based on an image you're failing to see.
When you look at yourself wear a smile they're free!
Then your beauty will blossom, like blooms on a tree.

Robert Chomany

You should be reminded every day
of the beauty that's in your heart,
no one can take that away from you,
because it is what sets you apart.
Be happy being you today,
and use the mirror that hangs on the wall,
to help you see who you really are
as you're standing proud and tall.

Tell me again why it is that you wait,
for an opportune moment or a particular date.
And tell me straight up why you *think* you should look
like that image created for a page in a book.
Your life is worth living starting right now today,
"There's no time like the present" is not just a cliché.

Robert Chomany

Years will come and years will go,
but as you look in the mirror you will find,
that when you believe in who you are,
the time will tend to be kind.

I'll bet when you look at yourself in the mirror
you see only what you think are flaws,
but what you are seeing are lines of laughter,
so smile as you remember the cause.
Look at yourself as others do,
and believe what they see is your grace,
then be yourself and own the moment,
you are here to create your own space.

Robert Chomany

Don't ever be ashamed to be who you are
be proud of your light and your looks,
your beauty's not based on society's whims
or an image in yesterday's books.
Put on your happy, and get in your groove
you should start every day feeling good,
smile today from the inside out
you don't have to impress, but you could.

Those who behold their true inner beauty
find an image that will never be clearer,
it's the first thing they see and the last thing as well
whenever they look in the mirror.
You'll know when you see it the first time I'm sure
and then it will always be there.
The essence of light in the depths of your soul
is the beauty of life, not the glare.

Robert Chomany

Don't smile today for the sake of others
smile today for you,
believe you are ready to take on the world
and be the best at whatever you do.
The very first person you should see every day
who matters the most overall,
is the one in the mirror who reflects who you are
the one who will answer your call.
When you smile today at the universe
use a smile right from your heart,
the world is ready to take you on,
and you're ready now to start.

Robert Chomany

Face the Fear

To face the fear, any fear, we must first recognize what it is we are actually afraid of.

Fear that keeps us out of dangerous situations is healthy, or sometimes a fear may be a phobia—fear of spiders, heights, or darkness. If worked on over time, phobias can be reduced to tolerable discomforts.

We must then ask ourselves if fear is coming from an unwillingness to accept change. Fear of change is a much more difficult challenge to overcome. You must admit to yourself that you're feeling unwilling to grow or move forward, and this inner dialogue is no easy task. You might fear leaving something you have grown comfortable with for something new: a new job, a new relationship, a new home, or even a new restaurant with an unfamiliar menu. If you make a conscious choice to start expanding your boundaries and limits, it's easier and a little less scary to adapt to change. If, on the other hand, someone else forces the change and it is out of your control, it can be overwhelming and terrifying. When we don't know what to expect, how can we prepare for the outcome?

If we choose to look at change as positive, even when it's out of our control, any outcome can be a good one. The thing is, when we let go of our fear, the change we were afraid of can become something to look forward to.

It can help to explore the possibilities of change—spend some time reflecting on where you've been and what you've done. Consider what a change may bring: new places, new faces, new adventures. A different job might mean an exciting career development, or the opportunity to move forward in a positive way. As with all things in life, how we look at options and choices, our perception of and approach to each fork in the road, determines how changes affect us. Perhaps someone with a fear of spiders will never be able to look at them in a positive way, but maybe simply acknowledging the fear is a positive thing—in knowing your fear, you know your strengths and weaknesses.

If it's fear that stops you from moving forward, find out why. Ask yourself, "What am I actually afraid of?" Most often, the answer will help you decide how to best handle whatever it is about change you truly fear.

Never give up and never let go
of a dream or a goal you desire,
never let fear ever hold you back
from that to which you aspire.

Robert Chomany

So you start your day in a relative way
to all the days before,
but today you hear a different knock
and you see a brand new door.
It's up to you to wander through
and have a little look,
don't be scared if you're not prepared
for a change that's off the hook.
Look inside and you will see
the you that you need to be,
that door appeared and opened wide
to finally set you free.

A new task looms and it's got you uneasy
you're not sure if you'll get it done,
it's not hard to do, just different for you,
it's not what you'd call fun.
Put out the fire that is the fear
you can smother it with a smile,
the courage you have to get things done
is part of your unique style.

Challenges will come from all directions
and some may catch you off guard,
but don't let the worry of what's unknown
make the easy things seem hard.

Walk not with ardent expectations
along an unknown trail,
instead be happy that you are able
to enjoy what might prevail.

Don't be afraid to express how you feel
a no won't an enemy make,
you have the free will to choose what is right,
and always what's best for your sake.

The news that we read, the things that we hear,
shouldn't shape who we are and grip us in fear.
The ways of the world are balanced each day,
the light and the dark, the work and the play.
For every sad story and all the gloom in the news,
there are good things that happen just out of our view.

Robert Chomany

Do you ever feel small while you're trying to BE,
like you quietly blend into the earth?
Do you ever feel you aren't recognized
for all that you are worth?
The power you have to stand out in a crowd
is in the energy you keep bottled inside,
the best way to be as big as you want
is to share your well-deserved pride.

Colorful feathers will do you no good
if you're always too scared to fly,
and you'll never be better at being yourself
if you don't take the chance to try.

Robert Chomany

Yes I know it's been said before
these words are nothing new,
but in case a reminder may be required
you need to believe in you.
Wake each morning and feel refreshed
don't greet the day with a yawn,
never fear the mirror's image,
instead say, "Bring it on."

Smiles in the WI:)ND

Find Peace

*H*ow do we find peace? Where can we look? Is it a thing, or a thought? When you are surrounded by serenity, do you feel peaceful? And if so, why? People under a great deal of stress are often prescribed the simple cure of finding some peace for a couple of minutes a day, with the goal of extending it to longer periods of time. Simply sitting back in your chair, closing your eyes, and tuning out the world for even a minute can produce the effects of soothing balance.

Peace is both a word and a state of being, a thought and a thing. Peace can be a familiar sound or smell; it resides in our minds and in our hearts. To find it we must not look. To see it we must not use our eyes. How then, can we be peaceful?

That's easy. We simply let it be. We leave the stress and struggles behind, and move forward into the peace and tranquility we are capable of producing with only our thoughts.

Clear-flowing streams, white fluffy clouds in a blue sky, a warm breeze that caresses—these are real, tangible things that inspire peaceful thoughts outside of society's concrete jungles. Most often, even urban jungles have places where you can go to experience serenity. You might fancy heading out of the city on an adventure, a quest, seeking peace. Hide from the stress of the world by finding a patch of green grass where you can lie down and gaze at the changing shapes of the clouds above.

It's important to "find peace," but it's not something you find by actively looking; you will more likely find it by letting yourself be. It exists all around you. Let it wrap you up in its calming energy. Seriously, right now, close your eyes and let yourself feel peace, then you will find it. It's not something you can hold in your hands, but if you relax your grip on life, your hands will become open to accepting it.

<blockquote>
Find your peace by letting life be,
explore the welcomed quiet,
if you let your mind be aware of serenity,
then your spirit is sure to buy it.
</blockquote>

Robert Chomany

The morning sun climbs so quietly
in a sky that's breathtakingly blue,
then touches upon an opening rose
that's been kissed by the glistening dew.
The essence of life begins to awaken
the moment that dawn makes her way,
take a moment this morning to just be still
and enjoy this part of the day.

Smiles in the WI:)ND

Robert Chomany

We seek to find our inner peace when all along it's there, hiding behind the warmth infused in all the smiles we share.

The calmest peace you will ever find
is the peace within your own heart,
it creates a rhythm in every breath
and has been there from the start.

Robert Chomany

Where is your euphoria? Does it really exist for you?
Is there a place you like to go and find peace in all you do?
Do you have the means to see the glow that happiness creates?
Can you feel the calm that a smile can share
and the warmth it often makes?
You need a place where you feel safe
away from society's stress,
a place that fills your soul with calm
so you can worry less.

Serenity comes from that place where you go
to find beauty and calm in yourself,
where living and life come together as one
and ego gets placed on a shelf.
Embrace the feelings of harmony
and your thoughts will all become sound,
the negative energy of worries and doubt
will no longer be easily found.

Robert Chomany

If ever you find your peace distraught
and you need to thwart life's guile,
close your eyes and find your balance
then calmly share a smile.
When you let yourself be surrounded by calm
you will experience the serene,
what some of us spend our entire lives seeking
you will finally have seen.

The essence of tranquility is there for us all
the trick is not to look,
it lives in the swirl of incense smoke
or the pages of a well-written book.
Don't be afraid to admit you are tired
or you're stressed and just need a break,
after giving your all you may need a rest,
which is good for you to take.

Robert Chomany

Downtime, meditation, or perhaps a nap
we all need to de-stress for a while,
to help put the happy back in our hearts
and the brightness back in our smiles.

The intricate patterns in life that occur
most often they're all overlooked,
we tend to not notice the beauty of things
because we're too overbooked.
Stress is a killer, it will wear you down
till you've got no strength left to smile.
Take a moment today, or five would be better,
to enjoy being you for a while.

Step out into nature and take in the beauty
you'll find that simplicity abounds.
While appreciating all of the sights you see,
enjoy the way silence sounds.

Wherever you go to find balance within
it's a place you are welcome to be,
your soul will spare no effort at all
to make sure you're safe and free.

Robert Chomany

Move Forward

*J*ust one step will move you forward into a new journey, perhaps an adventure. Just one step is the beginning of the rest of your life. "Moving forward" is one of the most familiar expressions these days. As a result of the deadlines and pressures of day-to-day living, we are often asked and sometimes even forced to move forward, to drop the things that are holding us back, things like attention to detail or need for closure.

Sometimes the process of letting go is what ultimately helps us carry on. If you are on an unfamiliar path and have a lesson to learn, by stepping off this path too soon, you risk losing the meaning of the lesson, the reason or purpose for it. While letting go and moving forward is always the eventual goal, keep in mind that sometimes it's healthy and helpful in the long run to stay with the more challenging lessons awhile; they show us a different way of looking at things.

Although this may sound strange, we can actually stand still while moving forward at the same time. Let your mind take over as you wind down at the end of the day. Let your thoughts turn to breathing in some fresh air, going home and relaxing, or playing a round of golf, perhaps. Let your thoughts move you forward from the confines of the office to the next step of your day. You can get back to living in the moment when the moment becomes calm and balanced.

The best way to move forward is with a positive outlook on life. Advance toward a place or space that fosters happiness and success by surrounding yourself with happy, successful people—not necessarily financially or professionally successful, but happy-with-their life, content-with-their-surroundings successful. Those who are full of positive energy can organically help you feel positive about yourself, then move that happy energy into tomorrow. Consider new desires and dreams, grab hold of something you haven't thought of before, move toward a place that allows you a clear view of where you've come from, with sights on the positive place you're moving forward to.

> With just one step an adventure begins,
> a journey to somewhere new,
> a place you have never been before,
> and a place that is perfect for you.

How does each day begin for you?
Does it start with a slate that is clean?
Or do you wake up in yesterday,
where your mind has already been?
Try if you will to end each day
feeling good about all that you've done,
and put on a smile when you wake in the morning
because a new day has just begun.

Robert Chomany

Start each day fresh by looking outside
and welcoming what will be.
Open the doors with those negative locks
by using your positive key.

We should take to the future only positive light,
leave darkness behind and it returns to the night.

Robert Chomany

Long is your shadow in the rising sun
it precedes you wherever you go,
if it's forward you're moving
your shadow recedes and then your smile can show.
When it's dusk once again your shadow does trail
it follows you now at length,
this journey you're on and the lessons you learn
are the things that give you your strength.

Robert Chomany

The choices you make and the directions you go
are determined by how much you believe
in the person who smiles back at you
from a mirror that will never deceive.

A new day will come and another one too,
and each will be different as it unfolds for you.
It will come with a sunrise full of color and light,
and chase evening away until it's well out of sight.

Robert Chomany

Let your energy flow without effort,
like a river that carves out its banks
while not forgetting the beauty of living
for this you should always give thanks.
Move your mind, your body, and your soul every day,
seek out new chances to grow;
a heart that is happy will always produce
a smile you're willing to show.

Robert Chomany

Each dawn you experience is an opportune chance
to play your own drum and create a new dance.
Don't dwell on those steps that you're used to taking
enjoy being you and the new moves you're making.

Robert Chomany

A path might not be what you expect
it might seem quite obscure.
Some are brand new with incredible views
and others have a history for sure.
The path you walk is a choice you make
and the effort it takes all depends,
on just how badly you want what's there
when the journey finally ends.

Often you have to take a step back to see
where your next step forward will take you.

Robert Chomany

The steps that you take to get where you're going
are all different and quite unique,
one step at a time, you learn as you go
the secrets to that which you seek.
Look at your life on each new stair,
where you've been and what lies ahead,
what once appeared as a wrinkle of doubt,
is now a confident smile instead.

Wherever you're going it's a journey you take
you should never feel it's for naught,
revel in the moments and memories you make
and enjoy the peace you have sought.

Robert Chomany

Your life is a path on which you walk
with directions only you can choose,
if your choice is always to believe in you,
you'll find you can never lose.

Robert Chomany

I send a smile to the world today
a smile that's full of hope,
a smile to help solve problems,
or provide the strength to cope.
I send a smile in the wind today
a smile that's sent with care,
it rides the wind until you get it
and now it's yours to share.
Take a moment to pass it on
and put it back out there,
send a smile from within your heart
just like the one you wear.

WI:)ND

Smiles in the WI:)ND

Communication

The ability to communicate is fundamental in this world, and yet, this ability is one of the hardest to truly master. For example, we can send a text or an email but not convey the feeling behind it, or we can speak eye to eye with someone but choose not to be honest. We often speak without communicating what we really mean or feel.

We humans have millions of words to convey information—words that enhance meaning or change perspective, words that we color or butcher. Sometimes we search for the right words, but other times we communicate how we are feeling by being silent. We also communicate with our bodies, like the animals with which we share our world. They use no words and yet we know what they are feeling or thinking most of the time. In the same way, we can see what a person is feeling or thinking from across the room. Something as subtle as a shift in posture expresses a change in energy with surprisingly clear impact.

Some forms of communication don't need to be explicitly taught. I've seen kids mimic their parents' expressions, not quite sure what they mean or when to use them, but using them to good effect just the same. Arms crossed, bottom lip out, head down—yep, that's one unhappy little person. This was a behaviour watched and remembered, not taught. It was communicated to them and they understood.

Do you take time to share your feelings with those who are close to you? Do you tell them you love them? Do you exchange a hug or a soft kiss when you greet? Love is certainly one of the easiest feelings to communicate, and yet it is perhaps the least expressed. We fall into habits of thinking they know, or coming up with excuses: "I'm at work," or "Not in public." People, if you love someone, show it today—tomorrow may not come. Hold hands, share warm smiles, speak the words, express your feelings. Share your day, discuss an idea, talk to friends about life or quietly sit with them and share energy, but in all these things, communicate how you feel. This ability is what keeps us real.

Take some time today to communicate with the world. Share who you are and why you are here; walk in a park and enjoy the outdoors, say good morning to a tree. What—are you uncomfortable talking to trees? They are life, they have energy. Or how about you ask a dog how it's doing and feel the response? A dog may not understand the words, but if you communicate your intent of kindness, it will respond with a gesture of acceptance: a tail wag, a lick, or in some cases even a smile. To really live life you need to communicate with all life, to share the world with all that exists and speak to all living things. Let your energy fill a room, shine your light in darkness, declare your intention of accepting all that is, simply because it is.

Never take this ability for granted; never underestimate the power of communication. Words can invite kindness and healing, or hurt and despair. We have the choice to speak freely and voice opinions—we also have the ability to listen, and the wisdom to know when to do either. All living things use the tool of communication to share in the absolute beauty of living. So live today, and feel free to use the simplest forms of communication: share a smile with a human or an animal, wave at a passing raven, or wink at yourself in the mirror and enjoy being you.

Enjoy life.

Communicate your feelings today
and take notice of what's going on,
connect yourself with all the wonders
that come with the new day's dawn.

Robert Chomany

When you chat with yourself from time to time
you can ask yourself questions too,
often the answers that present themselves
are the perfect solutions for you.

Smiles in the WI:)ND

Robert Chomany

Texts are handy and email too
but both can have quite a cost,
words alone won't express your feeling
the emotion is easily lost.
Don't be afraid to pick up the phone
it helps to clear the air,
use your voice to set the tone,
of what it is you need to share.

If thoughts must be shared without physical presence,
then think of how they'll be read.
Translate those thoughts that you've spent time thinking,
into good energy with a smile instead.

Robert Chomany

Rather than saying just yes or no
share the knowledge in your head,
if you share the thought of a crimson sky
use your words to paint it red.
The wisdom you share can become a direction
using words that you will speak,
for those who listen to what you say
may find a path to what they seek.

Don't be afraid to convey what you're thinking,
you're allowed to have an opinion,
enjoy being you and having your say,
you're not here to be anyone's minion.

Robert Chomany

Communicate because you can,
use your words you have the power,
you needn't go your entire life saying
less than a silent flower.

We will often keep feelings pent up inside
the stress eats us up and we swallow our pride.
Do what feels right and be happy you're you,
be one of the many don't hide with the few.
Life is so fleeting why bottle things in?
Express what you feel, shout out from within.

Robert Chomany

Today someone will think of you
your image will cross their mind,
at any given point in time
the thoughts of two minds can align.
Wherever you are, whatever you're doing,
another is going to share
that positive energy your soul emits,
as you're just standing there.

Your soul is your energy, your essence, your light,
which will flow for lifetimes to come,
it will be embellished and embraced by many
while it is seen and felt by some.
There are those who have walked before us in time
and are still with us in spirit today
now and then when you're in the right space
you can feel what they have to say.

Robert Chomany

A person who lives in the happiness of every moment
should share with the universe what they feel,
while standing in a group of a thousand souls
or being one with nature, enjoying what's real.

Robert Chomany

Sharing

Before you can share who you really are, you must first overcome the desire to hide parts of yourself. Of course we all have pasts, and parts of pasts we feel are not necessary to share, but does your ownership of certain skeletons define who you are? Or do the things you choose to share serve to raise your worth in comparison to someone else? How often have you heard someone reference a "lack of closet space" in a conversation to help improve their social status?

Often the feelings we share are directly connected to the things we possess, or we share the stress we feel when we don't have certain things. If we accept that we are merely sharing space with all other living creatures, then we can be comfortable sharing our things and the feelings behind them with others.

Sharing is what nature has done since the beginning of time. Fish and mammals share the water; plants and animals share the land. Nature is shared in perfect balance.

Every living thing shares with a purpose or plan; all things share the energy of life. But then we humans come along and decide what can and can't be shared, what is owned and what is not—which feelings are important enough to share and which are not. So many of us deem it necessary to own more of what nature leaves free.

We now have to buy water, pay for air, and fight for our little piece of dirt just so we can try to be happy. Sadly, after the fight, we are often too mentally exhausted to share our joy. Our cup is still half empty. The irony is that the little piece of earth we live on becomes the most valuable thing we can possibly share—because we can welcome friends into our home.

For the most part, physical things are just things. If you feel better owning them, then by all means, feel comfortable doing so, but you might consider accepting that they are *just things*. Simply share them and be happy being a part of nature. Once you do, it becomes clear that the most wonderful things you can ever own are your smiles, your opinions, and your light—no one else can ever take these things, no one else can ever own them, and you alone have the power to share them with the universe.

Share your heart, your smile, and your light.
Share with the world because it feels right.

Smiles in the WI:)ND

Last night I dreamed I shared a smile
in the wind like I always do,
it danced awhile among the clouds
then found its way to you.
Take it now and brighten your day
then send it out brand new,
to someone whom you've never met
who just might need it too.

Robert Chomany

Share your kindness, share your light,
share your inner glow,
share your love with furry friends
and they'll love you back you know.
Share the strength from within your soul
with those who need a lift,
know in your heart that your caring smile
can be the greatest gift.

Take a second in your life today to draw somebody near,
with a hug that says, while in this moment,
"There's nothing for you to fear."
A hug will show your empathy,
and means you have something to share
your strength from within, a gentle touch,
and the fact that you really care.

Robert Chomany

There's nothing that a hug can't fix
when it's given with kindness in mind
it takes away a negative day
and leaves a positive one behind.
Be sure to feel the energy in a hug that's shared with love
because those are hugs that are really special
they fit you like a glove.
When saying hello or a kind farewell,
a hug is your heart's extension,
from my point of view a hug from you
is a wonderful intention.

Robert Chomany

The things that mean the most to you
are the things you don't often share,
only the people who've walked on your path
will know those things are there.
We all have a history, a life that we've lived,
with memories and layers and such,
and quite often it's all the living we've done
that may interest another so much.
Take time to cherish the life that you have
it's the only one you will get,
surround yourself with positive souls
and appreciate those you've met.

Don't be afraid to stand up tall
and subdue your crippling pride
the easiest way to find your flow
is to calm what churns inside.

Robert Chomany

Sometimes you'll share something in your typical way,
but people will choose not to hear what you say.
Don't take it personally because listening is selective,
and some people you'll find can be arcane and protective.
Continue believing in what keeps your life real,
lead with compassion to show that you feel.

Your beauty is a part of the essence of you
it shines outward in all of the things that you do.
Share with the world your heart that is true
and be sure that your smile is the first thing they view.

Robert Chomany

It's okay to be humble, to share kindness and smiles,
and live your life happy as you add up the miles.
Hear while you listen then share what you know,
and keep your mind open so your spirit will grow.

Learn what you will, learn what you can,
learn about all that you find
learning is listening with more than your ears
learning is feeding your mind.
Learn to hear stories that elders share,
learn to then tell your own
learn to appreciate all of life's lessons
to share when your soul is full grown.

Robert Chomany

When you are asked, "What's new with you?"
is your answer always the same?
Do you reply with "Not much" and a shoulder shrug,
are you careful to avoid any blame?
Don't be afraid to share with the world
all the good things that happened today,
there will always be something that comes to mind
to express in a positive way.

Robert Chomany

Life is for living and living is sharing
from the lessons you've learned
to the smile that you're wearing.

Smiles in the WI:)ND

Friendship

Not much can be said about friendship that hasn't already been said many times over. Friendships keep positive and supportive energy flowing in the world. They make life easier and happier. Friends make our energy stronger.

What if we were to expand our boundaries a little? If you believe in soul mates, do you also believe in soul friends? Soul friend(s): a person who knows you inside and out; a mate who can make you smile from a thousand miles or two feet away; that particular companion who just knows when, wherever you are, you could use a hug or a smile sent special delivery in the wind. It's not a long stretch away from being real. It depends, I suppose, on how willing you are to accept or believe in something other than what society has taught you.

I believe that friends don't need to be human. Friends can have fur, feather, or fin; they can appear as trees, bees, or butterflies. Or we can be our own best friends—how many times have you been walking by yourself and felt perfectly at ease in your own company? Some friends can even be imaginary—why should children have all the fun? Friends might find us, or we might find them without ever looking; they just seem to happen.

As we travel our paths and enjoy our adventures, friends will come and go. Some will stay with us until our paths end, and others will be there for only an adventure or two. The beauty of a bond with a soul friend is that that person will always be there, and always only a thought away.

Remember, however, that to maintain a friendship, you must make the effort to share that smile, be it in the wind or in person. Remind your friends every now and then that you are thinking of them. It doesn't have to be every day or every week. The bond of a friendship isn't measured in time but in smiles shared. No matter how long it has been, when you meet with a soul friend once again, it will feel like only a heartbeat has passed since the last time you shared a moment together.

> Take with you on each new adventure
> the company of a friend,
> and you will find the memories made
> create smiles that never end.

Robert Chomany

Do you know what it takes to be part of a family
and not always family by birth?
It takes trust, support, and care when it's needed,
and never doubting your worth.

F eeling elated while
R ecalling those moments that
I nvolved a million laughs during
E ndless conversation about
N othing in particular till
D awn's wee hours with
S omeone special

Robert Chomany

Some friends you will find won't always be "on"
in fact some days they will fall off the earth.
But good friends when you need them will always be there,
and it's then that you will learn of their worth.

Some friends will always stand beside you
and some will have your back,
some will share your quirky traits
and some will keep you on track.
There are souls out there who will be your friend
with no conditions at all,
to help you see how awesome you are,
and pick you up whenever you fall.
The friends who share their hearts with you
are the ones who simply know,
that kindness shared needs not one word
it's in the smiles that they show.

Robert Chomany

Friends know a lot about your spirit
because that's just what they see,
not your size or shape or your style of clothing
they care more about your CHI.
They know when to talk and when to listen
they know how to boost you up,
they're not concerned with full or empty
they're just glad you have a cup.

Robert Chomany

Be thankful today for the friends you have
and for the friends you're soon to meet,
some you'll know by the smiles they share
the very first time you greet.
Some will have covers that help keep them warm
or blankets that wrap them up tight,
learn to be patient with these kinds of friends
it takes time to know them just right.

The energy you share in the wind with your friends
can be felt for a moment or two,
it can give them strength and lift them up
it can help them feel brand new.
Send a smile and a hug in the wind right now
to everyone you know,
you can then enjoy being you today
and feel your energy flow.

Robert Chomany

A friend of your soul has the same soul as you
and has been with you for lifetimes long past.
These friends, like the wind, will always share smiles
that are forged in the heart so they last.

Long-distance friends or folks that you've met
will remember your energy, and fondly I'll bet.
If the thoughts you are thinking are shared in the wind,
only a heartbeat will pass till you see them again.

Robert Chomany

We share our adventures as we put on the miles
and the journey continues as we share all our smiles.

Smiles in the WI:)ND

Tomorrow will come as it always does
and with it comes new hope,
that you will find the strength within
to help you grow and cope.
The silver edges that line the clouds
that now obscure your sun,
are the friends you have who will hold you close
until this day is done.

Robert Chomany

Tell yourself to share a smile and be happy being you,
tomorrow is just a day away and it always starts out new.

You might not think of how important you are
to someone that you know
until such time as the smiles you shared
no longer tend to show.
It's not just for the good old times
that we need to seek our friends,
but for times when we are down and out,
and would love some time to spend.

Robert Chomany

The world is full of all kinds of people
and some will stand out from the rest,
they are the ones who without being asked
will always give you their best.

A hug we'll share when we first greet.
"Till then," we say, "when next we meet."
The time it passes so very quick,
our schedules make it tough to stick.
The effort needed to make a call
is nothing compared to the fun overall,
so make the time to relax and live,
and share the light you love to give.

Robert Chomany

Differences

Does the thought of differences make you uneasy? We all experience differences in our day-to-day lives, but how do you handle them? They can be as ordinary and acceptable as, say, differences in how we commute. Bike, bus, car—we all have our own preferred modes of transit. But what about differences of opinion? Can you accept them? Do you need to be right all the time? Do you need the last word? Or do you shy away from confrontation? Do you keep your opinions to yourself?

Differences are healthy; they stem from the exchange of thoughts and ideas. In fact, a difference of opinion or in perception can help us see a totally new side of something and possibly enhance our creativity. The big question is, do you let a difference become an argument, and if so, does that argument get resolved? Firm beliefs and unalterable perceptions can be negative extensions of differences.

When controlled by both parties, however, arguments can produce a positive learning experience. Heated discussions convey deep passion surrounding a topic, as well as strength and conviction. Take the sky, for instance. It is unarguably blue, but arguments can arise if the shade of blue is questioned. "Sky blue" may not be a fitting enough answer for everyone, thereby creating the need for "azure."

You carve your own niche in the universe. You are unique, and so is your opinion. You are different; your thoughts are yours alone. Your ideas and perceptions, your belief in and understanding of things, your measurement of successes and lessons learned are different from anyone else's. Don't ever be ashamed of being different; instead, be proud to think the way you do and be the first to share thoughts. You never know just how positively your differences may be interpreted.

> To be different is to be unique and outstanding,
> not just one among the many
> so be proud to have a different idea,
> because without you there might not be any.

You won't please them all but you'll connect with a few,
and that's okay, it's your point of view.

Robert Chomany

Your opinion is yours be it silent or voiced,
you shouldn't let it be swayed,
no matter what others may think of your thoughts,
don't let yourself be played.

Smiles in the WI:)ND

Robert Chomany

There are many kinds of people with many thoughts and ways,
some might force their own ideas or have too much to say.
You can still be a part of the conversation
and acknowledge what you've heard,
a smile will work to show you're listening
if you're averse to finding the words.

Release the desire to criticize, and put away the hate,
learn to forgive because you can
there's more to life than fate.
Believe that you can make a difference by simply being you,
and soon the world will know you're there
because you're smiling too.

Robert Chomany

Take a moment and listen today
to what your heart is trying to say,
respect yourself because you care
about the world and what's out there.
Try as you might you soon will find
that people come in all different kinds,
some are strong and some are weak,
and some will help with what you seek.
Listen to those who are weathered and wise,
pay heed to those who compromise
believe in you and then you'll see,
you're in control of your destiny.

Hold on to something that makes you unique
some little thing you do
like the way that you smile with all of your heart
that thing's true to you.

Robert Chomany

You think you can see our differences
but we all breathe the same fresh air,
so look at the things that make us the same
and see first the smiles we share.

A single flower among many
will always remain as beautiful as it is meant to be.

Robert Chomany

From a soul that is yours and very unique
comes your spirit that helps you to see,
you're someone who belongs to the universe
and the someone you love to be.

Open your heart in a welcoming way
to all those who live on this earth,
no human should ever be given permission
to judge another soul's worth.

Robert Chomany

Each one is the same, each one is different,
each one has a life of its own,
each one has a name, each one belongs,
each one has a chance to be known.
Each one has its color, each one has its style,
each one has its reason to grow,
each one has its smell, each one has its beauty,
each one shares its subtle glow.

Beauty won't always be what you expect
but it's always there to behold,
it may be found in some words that you've heard
or in actions that may unfold.
Consider each day that what you believe
might not be what others will feel,
but the world needs balance so accept if you please
an opinion is part of the deal.

Robert Chomany

Compassion

Compassion is a response to others in need—and not just other human beings but all life. And not only life that is in dire need, but all life outside of your definition of happiness. A dog chained to a post, a plant drying up without water, a bird with a broken wing—any living thing at any point in time can trigger your compassion.

Compassion is positive energy. It can be seen by those who need it, it can be felt by those to whom it is offered, and it will be appreciated by all who receive it. It's a gift to be given and received. It comes from the heart and may begin as sympathy, but it can grow into a need to bring something or someone back to a place of comfort. Compassion is a desire to help all those within our power to help.

Those with compassionate hearts are often the softest to approach, but their resolve to limit suffering also indicates a fierce strength. Showing compassion towards all life opens your eyes to the idea of how others deserve to be happy with living.

It's important to remember, though, that compassion needs to reach inward and not just outward. The people who are most compassionate to others often neglect to show compassion to themselves. They become so wrapped up in the well-being of those around them that they lose touch with their own happiness, and this stress takes its toll. There must be balance. Share what you feel, feel with conviction, and then help within limits and boundaries set by you to maintain your own happiness. Don't let your compassion take from you your enjoyment of living.

We can't help the whole world, but we can mean the world to those we help.

> Take in a calm breath as you start your day
> and remember these words you've heard
> always treat others as you'd like to be treated
> and be the first to speak a kind word.

Smiles in the WI:)ND

There are many simple ways to make somebody's day:
an honest smile, a warm hello,
and something kind to say.
It's not a mystery or anything new
in fact it's just called caring,
human beings and animals too,
we all have smiles worth sharing.

Robert Chomany

Mother Nature creates with kindness and caring
and puts energy in all living things,
with hopes that the world will share in a dance
to the music the wind will bring.

Deliver a smile in the wind today
it's a smile you know will come back.
Wrap it with kindness for those who are down,
because it's a smile they lack.

Robert Chomany

Send out a heartfelt hug today,
and wrap it with great care,
send it out in the wind today
then look, it should be there.
The world should smile a whole lot more,
and send some hugs for free
it's up to us to make the world a better place to be.

Confidence comes when you practice just living
and compassion will follow when your heart does the giving.
Humility happens when you're at peace with your being
and a positive perspective produces smiles worth seeing.

Robert Chomany

There are no limits to the light in your soul
no lines or ceilings or doors,
there is an abundance of kindness instead
and an essence uniquely yours.
Share your smile with all that you have
and venture beyond your means,
find the strength within you today
to extend your positive gleam.

Kindness is something we all have inside
and we should use it on all living things,
but kindness is also required for you
just try it and see what it brings.
Believe in yourself and all that you do
believe in what you can achieve,
have faith in yourself and all that transpires
will be everything you can perceive.

Robert Chomany

For the sake of your soul be good to yourself
for the sake of the world be kind,
for the sake of your heart be good to your health
and for the sake of others unwind.

A kindness done for the sake of a smile
is the beginning of greater balance within.

Robert Chomany

Do you know what it means to have the means
to never have to be mean?
You can find the good in every scene by seeing
what needs to be seen.

Robert Chomany

Inspiration

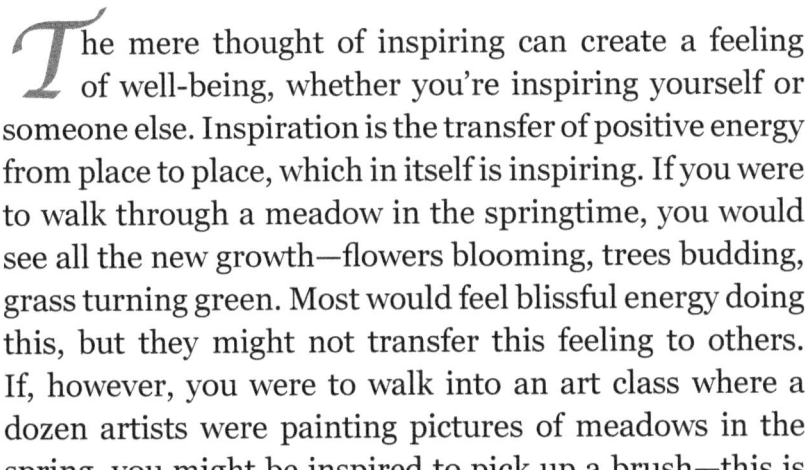

The mere thought of inspiring can create a feeling of well-being, whether you're inspiring yourself or someone else. Inspiration is the transfer of positive energy from place to place, which in itself is inspiring. If you were to walk through a meadow in the springtime, you would see all the new growth—flowers blooming, trees budding, grass turning green. Most would feel blissful energy doing this, but they might not transfer this feeling to others. If, however, you were to walk into an art class where a dozen artists were painting pictures of meadows in the spring, you might be inspired to pick up a brush—this is the transfer of positive energy in the form of inspiration.

Inspiration can come from something you read, something you see, or even something you feel. It is cause and effect in action. It can cause you to do something out of the ordinary, which in turn can inspire someone else to do the same, thereby creating a domino effect of good and positive energy.

What is most intriguing is the subtlety behind some inspiration. Did you know that a smile alone can inspire a person to become cheerful, or a nod of acceptance can inspire productivity? Something as mundane and effortless as holding a door open can inspire feelings of politeness and pride in both parties, and this could possibly make the day brighter for everyone else in the vicinity.

Inspiration should come at no cost; it should be natural to both give and receive. Energy-wise, received inspiration should weigh the same as sent inspiration. Once you are inspired, go with the flow, see what happens. And once you inspire others, leave it with them, let them enjoy it—no expectations. If you have a greater need, to inspire the universe, perhaps, then smile while doing it; the universe will always smile back. Having said that, don't look to the universe for inspiration unless you're strongly open to new opportunities. In other words, the inspiration the universe sends back could lead you to a totally different path—are you open to something completely different in your life?

> Life might seem good when life is planned
> but you need desire if it's lacking,
> you can take on the world without a hitch
> if you're inspired to just get cracking.

We all have routines when we get out of bed
to help us greet the day
a smile, the sunshine, and some inspiration
is always a positive way.

Robert Chomany

Inspiration will come in all forms
and it comes from a source that you choose,
maybe a quote from a page that you read
or even your very own muse.
Most important is the result you achieve
when you finally know what it takes,
to be inspired with what you have
and enjoy the changes you make.

Robert Chomany

It starts with a concept you create in your mind
which then turns into a smile,
before you know it a project is born
and it's one that may take you a while.
You can't imagine all the things you can do
until you give them a go,
when you're done, stand back and admire your effort
be proud of the work that you show.

Don't tell artists what colors to use
when it's time to paint the sky,
if they're watching the morning sun as it rises
they'll get it right first try.
Our minds are ours to use as we will
to create our own way of living,
and all the good things that come our way
are due mainly to the effort we're giving.

Robert Chomany

If you've ever wondered what you mean to the world
I'll tell you this right now,
there are people out there who look up to you,
and to them you're important somehow.
Whatever it is that makes you unique
is a gift that others might use,
the way you smile and share who you are
creates energy on which to muse.

Be happy being you today and every day that's new
share the ideas that create a smile and might inspire too.

Robert Chomany

You have followed paths that others walk
their footprints have been laid,
have you ever turned around to look
at the path which you have made?
Others will follow you as well to places you have been,
someone else will be inspired
by the things that you have seen.

Smiles in the WI:)ND

Robert Chomany

You need not follow like a little lost sheep
to get to wherever you're going,
you have your dreams and goals and desires
and a smile that's always worth showing.
Stand up, stand out, it's okay to be you,
be proud to be out in the lead,
get good at the things you like to do
if you're trying you're learning, and then you succeed.

Step up and inspire in a positive way
by putting on a smile that's bright,
think of the moon that hangs high in the sky
just happy to show off its light.

Robert Chomany

Smiles in the WI:)ND

A soul will truly begin to soar
when the wind is beneath its wings,
then with a smile it will dance in the clouds
for the happiness it brings.

Robert Chomany

Your strength comes from doing the
things at which you excel
your character comes from trying things
at which you do not.

Smiles in the WI:)ND

Be proud of you and what you do
create with your two hands,
don't live your life with an idle mind
be inspired where you stand.
Explore the things that make you think
see the things you need to see,
do the things that make you smile
be the you that you need to be.

Robert Chomany

I know the wind will carry a smile
I know this because it's true,
I sent a smile just yesterday and it ended up on you.
Imagine now if we all sent one
in the wind as it passes by,
can you see the world as a happier place
without even having to try?
Go ahead and put one on and send it in the wind from you
for anyone around the world so they can share one too.

Smiles in the WI:)ND

Acknowledgements

I would like to thank all those who have continually shown support and shared their energy and smiles with me along this journey.

And thank you to all the beautiful people who enjoy what I write. Without you, my words would remain simply unshared thoughts.

Smiles in the WI:)ND

Other titles
by Robert Chomany

Bawb's Raven Feathers, Volumes I-V

http://bit.ly/ROBERTCHOMANYauthor
www.bawbsravenfeathers.net

Connect with the author:

Facebook: http://www.facebook.com/rchomanyauthor
Instagram: http://www.instagram.com/bawbtheauthor

About the Author

Robert (BawB) Chomany is a writer and the author of several books: a series of five volumes titled BawB's Raven Feathers and this latest work, *Smiles in the WI:)ND*. Robert writes from his soul, and the words are translated by his heart to create word hugs—quotes of inspiration designed to help readers find themselves among the shadows.

The world can be a nasty place some days, and we all need to find our light, our smiles, and our energy to get through. Once we find our balance, we can share what we've learned and start spreading the happiness the world so desperately needs.

Robert was born and raised in Calgary, AB, and has spent a lifetime creating adventures, sharing smiles, and finding new ways to attract happiness. Whether he's walking in nature or riding his Softail, you'll always find him sharing a smile in the wind.

Smiles in the WI:)ND

www.ingramcontent.com/pod-product-compliance
Lightning Source LLC
Chambersburg PA
CBHW042112120526
44592CB00042B/2711